WELCOM

C000098239

ON BEHALF OF the worshipping community, I welcon
As you tour this remarkable church you can trace the layer   al,
reaching back to our foundation by St Wilfrid in c.674AD. In parts of the building you are
standing in Wilfrid's monastic cathedral, in others you enter the 13th-century Augustinian
priory, while the building as a whole, now the parish church of Hexham, tells the story of our
Christian life. This guide gives you a brief history, and then
from page 14 takes you on a journey around the Abbey,
describing the different parts of the church and pointing to
details and objects of particular interest.

This pre-Conquest chalice is displayed in the south aisle

Our worship of God encourages each and every
one of us along an adventurous journey of faith. I hope
that you will not only view the Abbey's treasures, but
also find calm and refreshment within its walls and walk
a step of faith. You are welcome to join us for a service or
leave your prayers in this place of peace. At times the
Abbey is also a place of great activity, filled with music, for
example, or interest in an exhibition, or the enthusiasm of an
educational visit. For me this animation is as much a joy as the
times of silence, for in such ways the Abbey continues its work
of enjoying, celebrating and sharing God's love.

I hope that long after your visit to Hexham
Abbey this guide will help to recall memories and offer
you something of God's peace, hope and love.

THE REVEREND CANON GRAHAM B. USHER
RECTOR AND LECTURER

The Resurrection of Christ, a wood panel painting which stands above the altar in the Leschman chantry chapel, is very unusual in showing Christ rising from a coffin. It also shows Prior Leschman kneeling in worship and the instruments of the Crucifixion, including cross, spear and dice

HISTORICAL TOUR

HEXHAM ABBEY, dedicated to St Andrew, is one of the earliest surviving Christian foundations in Britain and for much of its history has reflected two very different Christian lifestyles: the enclosed community of men living by a monastic rule and the open community of the faithful who come together regularly to share in acts of worship. Built in 674-8 as a Benedictine monastery, a centre for the spread of the Christian faith and place of pilgrimage, by the formidable Wilfrid, bishop of York, it almost immediately became a cathedral church when the huge see of York was divided into four in 681 - much to Wilfrid's disapproval - and Hexham became a bishopric. Wilfrid's monastery was damaged by Viking raids in the ninth century and was refounded as a priory for Augustinian canons in the 12th century, when the church was handsomely rebuilt as both a monastic and a parish church. Serving solely as a parish church after the dissolution of the monasteries, it was again substantially restored and rebuilt in the 19th and early 20th centuries to create the impressive and dignified building we see today.

*Celebrating communion
at the circular nave altar*

The church at Hexham originated in a substantial grant of land – the origin of the surrounding area of Hexhamshire, which remained a distinct county until the 16th century - made to Wilfrid in 674, by the Northumbrian queen Etheldreda, for the endowment of a monastery. Built on a spur of land looking east across the Tyne valley just below the point where the North and South Tyne rivers combine, the church was one of the first to be built of stone, on a magnificent scale and possibly to a Roman-style basilica plan which was unique in Britain at the time and could well have been inspired by Wilfrid's travels. Wilfrid's follower and biographer Eddius Stephanus described its 'crypts of beautifully dressed stone, the vast structure supported by columns of various styles and numerous side-aisles, the walls of remarkable height and length... we have never heard of its like this side of the Alps'.

LEFT: *The Abbey stands above a river crossing and dominates the surrounding area; it lay at the heart of the royal grant of land to St Wilfrid*

OPPOSITE: *Hexham Abbey from the east, showing the 19th-century east end and the 13th-century tower and transepts*

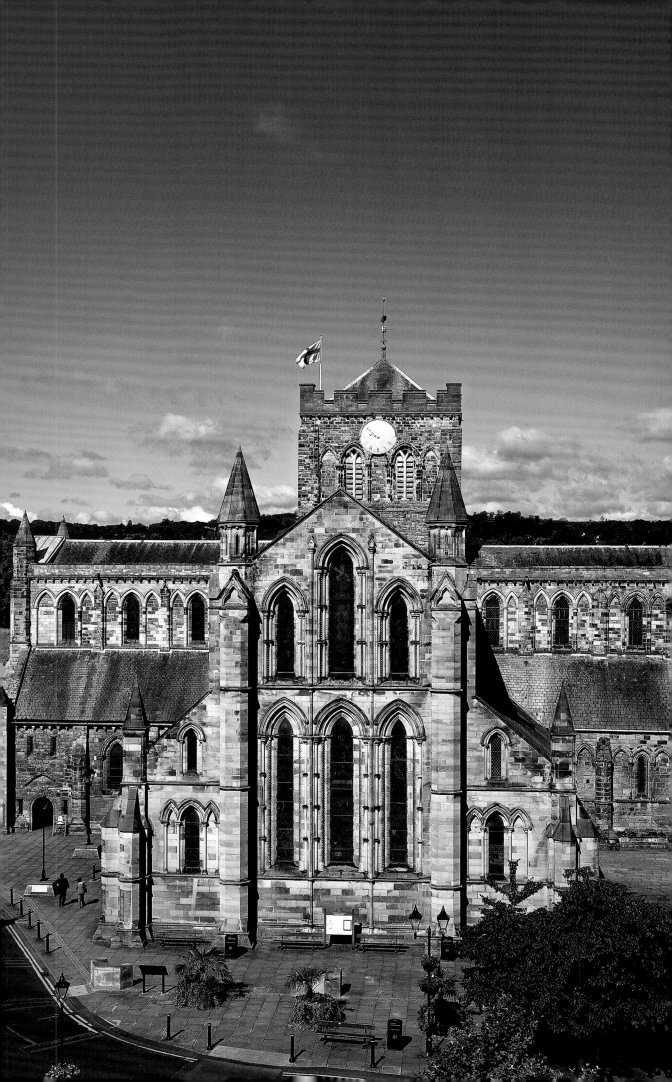

ST WILFRID AND THE EARLY CHURCH

WILFRID (634-709), the first native Saxon to become bishop of York, is one of the more forceful and memorable characters in the complicated story of the conversion of the Saxon kingdoms in seventh-century Britain. He was hailed by his biographer Eddius Stephanus as responsible for introducing 'the catholic way of life to the churches of the English'. The powerful northern king Edwin had converted to Christianity in 628 at the instigation of his wife, daughter of the Kentish king Ethelbert, who in turn had been baptised by the Roman missionary Saint Augustine. Wilfrid, a Northumbrian nobleman's son, was brought up as a Christian, served in the royal household and used his royal contacts to travel to Gaul and to Rome. But Edwin's successor Oswald, moving to re-establish the Christian faith after a period of disorder, looked west rather than south, to Celtic Christian Ireland and its monastic outpost on the island of Iona, where Oswald himself had been baptised. The 'Golden Age of Northumbria', the flowering of Christian culture which resulted from this confluence of cultural and religious influences, reflects the great wealth accumulated by the kings and nobles of this frontier kingdom; they became givers to the Church on a grand scale.

Tensions between the two strands of Christianity came to a head in 664 at a royal council, the Synod of Whitby, where Wilfrid, then abbot of Ripon, was spokesman for Roman practices and won the day over the Celtic church. This established him as a major player in both church and kingdom – he became bishop of York

in 669 – and embroiled him in the tricky politics of the time, for the rest of his life was fraught with quarrels, banishments and appeals to the Pope. The grant of land to Wilfrid for the Hexham church, effectively transferring a large estate from crown to monk, became a source of irritation to the king, particularly when Wilfrid encouraged the queen Etheldreda to enter the monastic life, and by 677 Wilfrid had been deprived of his bishopric and his property and expelled from Northumbria. This provided the new archbishop of Canterbury, Theodore, with the chance to break up the huge see of York. Wilfrid meanwhile travelled to Rome to enlist papal support – the first such appeal by an English ecclesiastic to the see of Rome - and in 679 a meeting of bishops found in his favour, but on his return to Northumbria to claim his rights he was again rejected. In 703, at the grand age of 69, Wilfrid was again in Rome, finally being granted his own foundations of Ripon and Hexham shortly before his death.

ABOVE: *The chapel of St Wilfrid in the north aisle of the chancel forms part of the rebuilt east end. It is reserved for private prayer and was dedicated in 1996*

LEFT: *The Frith stool, a Saxon cathedra or bishop's throne, one of only two surviving examples, which may well have been used by Wilfrid himself*

OPPOSITE: *St Wilfrid with his bishop's mitre and crozier, depicted on the 15th-century reredos which now stands in the chancel*

Wilfrid's church was an imposing building more than 35 metres (100 feet) long, standing on the site of the nave of the present church and consisting of a nave with one or more aisles on either side. The builders, probably brought in from the continent, made good use of the generous supply of worked stone at the old Roman fort at Corbridge, only three miles away. All that remains of the church today is the rare and unusual crypt; the foundations of an apse; some decorative Saxon stonework, including Acca's cross; re-used pieces of Roman masonry; and the Saxon Frith stool (see page 5), which may have served as Wilfrid's *cathedra* or bishop's throne. The crypt, with its small central room, vestibule and three entrances, provided an impressive ambience for the cult of saints' relics which was an important feature of the Anglo-Saxon church. The dedication to St Andrew suggests that Wilfrid may have brought back relics of the saint, perhaps pieces of cloth that had touched the saint's bones, venerated in the church of St Andrew in Rome where Wilfrid is known to have worshipped.

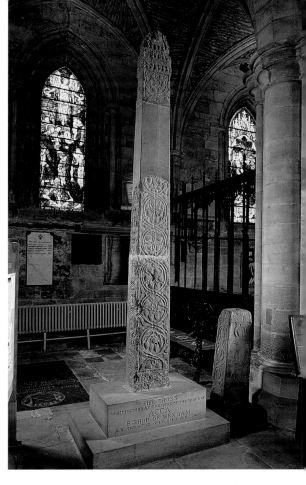

This eighth-century stone cross, known as Acca's cross, is carved with Christian motifs and is typical of the fine Northumbrian school of stonework. It is traditionally held to be the headstone marking bishop Acca's grave

This impressive structure was also from the beginning a major centre of Christian culture and learning, acting effectively both as the religious capital of the newly romanised Northumbrian church and as a focus of pilgrimage. Wilfrid introduced the Benedictine rule, with its emphasis on the study and copying of the Scriptures. His successor as abbot and bishop was his friend and companion Acca who, according to Bede's contemporary history of the English church, enriched the church with painting, sculpture and rich hangings, created a 'very complete and excellent library', and introduced a skilled music teacher to ensure that the music and liturgy of the church were as fine as any in Europe. The musical tradition continues today with the Abbey's various choirs and in services which also embrace contemporary music.

Hexham remained a religious and cultural centre for some time after Wilfrid's death, but gradually the power of the Northumbrian kingdom began to wane and Norse raiders became increasingly bold. Around 821 Hexham ceased to serve as a cathedral and at some point the

This steep stone stair leads down from the modern nave to the Saxon crypt, the only structural part of Wilfrid's church to survive

monastery was abandoned, but the church, and the settlement around it, survived, with a single hereditary priest. In about 1083 the then priest, Eilaf, obtained a grant to rebuild the church from the Norman archbishop of York and by the early 1100s the archbishop had established a body of canons at Hexham to restore both the religious community and the church. One of the famous sons of Hexham during this time was Aelred, later to become abbot of Rievaulx Abbey in North Yorkshire and a spiritual writer, whose father was the keeper of Hexham's shrine.

BELOW: *The choir process up the nave at the start of a service, in a musical tradition begun by bishop Acca*

RIGHT: *The early 20th-century baptistry window, at the west end of the nave aisle, shows scenes from the history of English Christianity: on the left, the baptism of the Kentish king Ethelbert by Saint Augustine; in the centre, Pope Gregory the Great with Anglian children in the slave market in Rome; and on the right, Queen Bertha praying for Ethelbert's conversion*

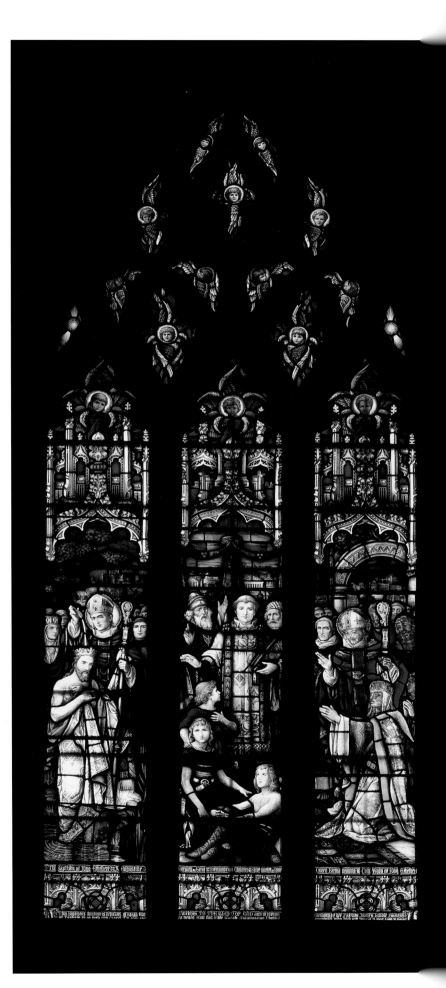

AUGUSTINIAN CANONS AND LIFE IN A PRIORY

The Augustinian canons developed as a separate religious order in the 11th century as part of the more general ecclesiastical reform movement. Like monks, they lived an enclosed and regulated life and celebrated divine office - the daily services of the church - but, unlike monks, they were active in the local community. At Hexham their leader was a prior, and their community was called a priory.

The canons' day was punctuated by the celebration of seven church services, starting soon after midnight. For this first service, they would come straight from their dormitory, across a vestibule above where the Abbey Shop now stands, and down the night stair directly into the

The celebration of the eucharist remains at the heart of Christian observance today

church. For all other services they entered the church from the doorway at the foot of the night stair, now sealed. Two of these services, Matins and Vespers (which we call Evensong) are still regularly celebrated today. As well as the daily rhythm of communal prayer, psalm-singing and the celebration of the eucharist, the canons were committed to practical good works among the local people, serving in parish churches, teaching, and caring for the sick and needy – all still part of the work of the parish clergy and lay ministers.

These decorative arches are all that remain of the lavatorium in the west walk of the cloister, where the monks would wash before entering the refectory to eat

The canons rebuilt the monastic buildings, adding an enclosing precinct wall and a gatehouse through it from Gilesgate. The lower storey of the gatehouse, now called St Wilfrid's gate, can still be seen, but little remains of the rest. Monastic buildings in western Europe were for hundreds of years built to a standard plan with an arcaded courtyard or cloister at its heart, serving as both a haven from the outside world and an efficient and sheltered link between the various functional buildings. At Hexham the cloister stood to the south of the church and traces of its arcading can be seen on the western wall of the south transept.

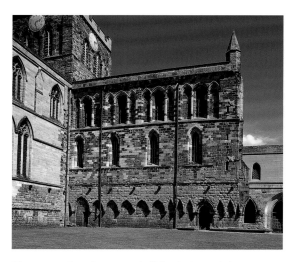

The tower and south transept, built by the Augustinian canons in the 13th century, showing traces of the cloister arcading at ground level; the cloister was the centre of domestic monastic life

The rebuilding of the church began almost at once but it seems that in about 1180 the plan was revised and enlarged, without changing the layout of the cloister and slype. Normally the slype, the passageway leading to the outside world, would have been outside the church but here, unusually, it forms the end bay in the enlarged south transept. Clearly by 1180 the canons were well-established at Hexham and confident enough to undertake a major building programme, for between about 1180 and 1250 they constructed a substantial church, a fine example of the new Early English style, with its combination of solid stonework, multiple pillar shafts, pointed arches and rich decoration. The aisled rectangular chancel was built first; then the south transept; the more richly ornamental north transept; and the crossing, which linked these three arms of the church under a solid tower. We know from documentary sources that various starts were made on replacing the dilapidated Saxon remains of the fourth arm, the nave, but there is little evidence to show what was achieved apart from the layout.

The night stair and the soaring lancet windows of the south transept, built by the canons in the Early English style

BENEDICTINE AND AUGUSTINIAN SPIRITUALITY

The Rule of St Benedict has shaped monastic living for 1500 years, with its motto of *'pax et ora et labora'*, peace and prayer and work. Benedict, disenchanted with his times, sought the life of a hermit. When others came to him for guidance, he taught them to seek God together in tightly-knit communities with a common prayer and a contemplative lifestyle. As a guide for these communities, the Rule of St Benedict begins with an invitation: 'Listen'. Listen to the voice of God in your hearts, in the community and in the Bible. The Rule continues to this day to inspire women and men to live, pray and be challenged by its pattern of life.

The Augustinian, or Austin, canons lived by the rule of the fourth-century St Augustine of Hippo, thought to be the oldest monastic rule in the western Church. It is characterised by reflection, prayer and mission and became increasingly popular in the 11th and 12th centuries. Its ethos may be summed up as 'love and learning'; the search for truth through study,

alongside a life of affection and fairness to others. Augustine taught that we meet God at the centre of our beings and in that encounter we come to know ourselves more deeply.

The worn treads of the night stair are testimony to the devotion of generations

The Leschman chantry chapel commemorates a 15th-century prior; its delicate wood tracery contrasts with the crude and sometimes comical vigour of the stone carving below

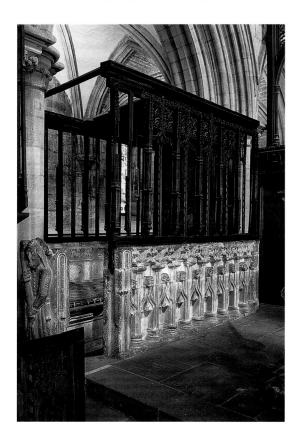

After a long period of relative peace, the disputed succession to the Scottish throne embroiled Tynedale and the rest of the borders in war, and in 1296 the priory and much of the town was set alight by raiding Scots led by William Wallace – the lead that fell from the roof can still be seen on some areas of the Abbey's floor. As part of the 14th-century renewal of the church, a row of low chapels was built at the east end across the width of the chancel and aisles, and soon another start was made on the nave, for Newcastle merchant Roger Thornton left a bequest for building work in his will dated 1429.

The most impressive survival from this period, however, is the assembly of furnishings with which the church was enriched during the 15th century. By this time faith had become a more individual concern; rather than general endowments to religious foundations, benefactors founded chantry chapels, where prayers could be said in perpetuity for the welfare of their souls, and

commissioned elaborate tombs. At Hexham the Ogle and Leschman chantry chapels were inserted into the chancel aisles, the latter particularly rich in carved stonework and delicately worked wood

The choir stalls in the chancel are also elaborately and humorously carved

tracery. Elaborate oak stalls or sedilia were placed in the sanctuary for the use of the officiating clergy and decorated stalls added in the choir for the canons. Sequences of wood panel paintings showing the story of Christ's Passion, the early bishop-saints of Hexham and, a fine and unusual survival, the Dance of Death, testify to the church's teaching role at a time when the great majority of the congregation would have been illiterate.

Finally, early in the 16th century, a splendid wooden screen was erected to separate the chancel from the congregation in the nave – which was therefore clearly in use at the time. Soon after, however, came the break with the church in Rome and the establishment of a separate protestant Church of England, with the king, Henry VIII, as its head. In 1536, when the commissioners charged with closing the priory arrived, the canons initially resisted them with a brave show of force. In February 1537, however, the priory was formally dissolved. The younger canons were simply thrown out; the older ones were given a gown and forty shillings each.

One of a series of 15th-century wood panel paintings, now in the north aisle of the chancel, depicting Christ's Passion; here he shoulders the cross

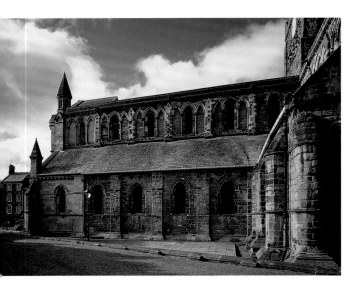

The chancel from the north-west, across the old graveyard, showing the original 13th-century aisle wall with clerestory above, and the final bay and turret at the east end which was rebuilt in the 19th century

The priory church survived as a parish church in the care of a single curate, while the former priory buildings became the residence of the Lord of the Manor. The Allendale family, the Abbey's lay rectors then and now, had the right as patrons to appoint the rector to the living. In 1625 the Worshipful Company of Mercers, a City of London livery company, received a bequest from the estate of Richard Fishborne to establish Puritan lectureships and Hexham was one of the locations selected. The Mercers' Company continued to appoint lecturers to preach sermons regularly in the Abbey, but since 1902 the position of rector and lecturer have been vested in the same person.

Gradually the remnants of the nave were abandoned - by the 18th century the area had become a burial ground - while various records survive of minor repairs to the rest of the fabric. By 1830 the east end too was in a precarious state and in 1858 it was dismantled and replaced with a design based on what remains of Whitby Abbey. Some of the stained glass also dates from the second half of the 19th century; sadly, only fragments of medieval glass have been found.

Finally, at the end of the 19th century, a

This 19th-century painting shows the tower and chancel surrounded by housing which obscures the transepts, before the reconstruction of the east end or the building of Beaumont Street

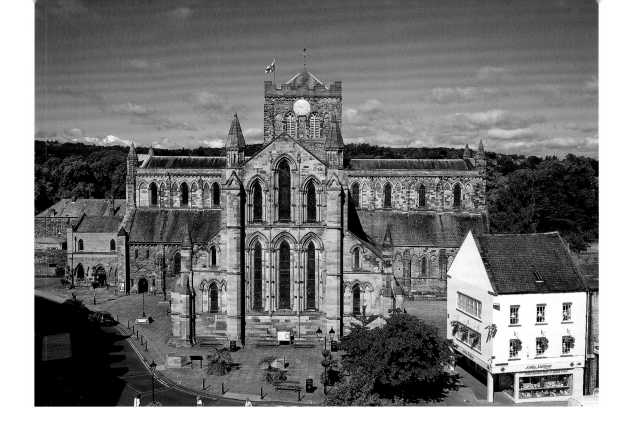

particularly energetic rector, the Rev. E.S. Savage, persuaded Newcastle steel magnate Thomas Spencer to pledge a £12,000 donation to rebuild the nave on the existing 12th-century plan. The architect was Temple Moore, a pupil of Sir George Gilbert Scott. Like his mentor, Moore built in a Victorian Gothic style, but one subtly and deliberately different from the medieval original. The new nave was finished in 1908. Finally, after more than 1200 years, the church that Wilfrid founded as a centre for evangelism again stood complete, a testament, in its more modest capacity of parish church, to the resilience of the Christian faith.

That dynamic sharing of faith which Wilfrid brought to this place so long ago continues with the life of the church community today. In the 21st century Hexham Abbey remains a place of interest for visitors, a resting place on life's journey and a place where pilgrims can encounter God. Church members, together with ecumenical friends, share in providing inspiring educational visits for school groups, bringing the history and the faith of the building alive. The holy space offered by the church is used for traditional liturgy as well as contemporary worship, and for the life events of baptisms, weddings and funerals. Local people come here for gatherings such as art exhibitions and concerts. Above all Hexham Abbey continues to be a place where life, faith and learning can flourish.

ABOVE: *The Abbey from the east today*

BELOW: *The window in the south transept, showing Christ blessing the children, is by noted 19th-century designer Henry Holiday, who set up his own stained-glass studio*

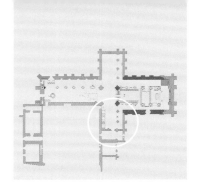

WALKING TOUR

The well-worn steps of the night stair are still used for services today by the choirs as they process from the Song School across the gallery and down into the church. The choirs continue a musical tradition begun by Wilfrid's successor, Acca

YOU ENTER THE CHURCH by a passage known as the SLYPE which, unusually, forms the final bay of the south transept, and once linked the cloister and the monastic buildings to the south of the church with the world outside. As you turn right from the slype into the south transept, the immediate view is dramatically dominated by the great pointed arches of the crossing and the soaring lancet windows of the north transept beyond. The great windows and natural lighting reflect the confident spirituality of its builders.

The SOUTH TRANSEPT was built in a relatively short period of about ten years and finished c.1230, soon after the chancel. Standing in the entrance, you can see that the wall to your left is considerably less ornamented than that to the right; perhaps the canons were in a hurry to finish their sheltered entrance. The most immediately striking feature here, one of the finest monastic survivals in an English church, is the NIGHT STAIR on your left which leads down from a gallery over the slype. The gallery once gave access to the canons' dormitory, allowing them to move under cover into the church to sing the night offices.

BELOW: The Roman tombstone at the foot of the night stair shows the dedicatee, the standard-bearer Flavinus, in plumed helmet and on horseback, trampling a defeated but still aggressive Briton under his horse's hooves. The inscription tell us that Flavinus had already served for seven years in the Roman army when he died aged 25

At the foot of the night stair, and placed in front of the sealed entrance which would once have been the canons' processional route from the cloister, is a ROMAN TOMBSTONE which was re-used in Wilfrid's church and may have come originally from the Roman military cemetery at Corbridge. It is dedicated to the memory of Flavinus, a *signifer* or standard bearer, who died aged 25 towards the end of the first century AD, early in the Roman occupation of Britain and before the building of Hadrian's Wall. Opposite the night stair is a chapel dedicated to Wilfrid's patron St Etheldreda, who made the original grant of land on which the monastic church was built; this is set aside for prayers concerning contemporary world issues.

OPPOSITE: View from the gallery above the night stair, showing the complex internal layering of the south transept at the right, with the crossing arches and the light-filled north transept to the left

RIGHT: *The Spital cross, showing the Crucifixion on the main face and a tightly angled view of the vine scroll on the other three faces*

Beyond the chapel are the worn remains of two imposing carved stone crosses, examples of a richly creative and uniquely Anglo-Saxon expression of faith. The taller one is known as ACCA'S CROSS (see p.6), as it is traditionally held to be the headstone that documentary sources tell us marked bishop Acca's grave – although it may rather have served as the marker for a place of worship before a church was built. Certainly the decoration is typically eighth-century, with its intricate, twining vine pattern, which recalls both the Mediterranean roots of Christianity and Christ's words in John 15: 'I am the vine and you are the branches. Those who abide in me and I in them bear much fruit.' The more damaged SPITAL CROSS (it was found near the site of the medieval Hospital of St Giles) has a similar vinescroll tracery on three faces, with a representation of the Crucifixion on the main one.

As you turn right into the south aisle of the chancel, a glazed niche in the wall on your right holds an ANGLO-SAXON CHALICE, found in a coffin in the transept when heating pipes were being laid in the 1860s. A rare survivor, probably from the tenth century, this held the communion wine, but was possibly used for taking the eucharist out into the community, as it is too small to serve a congregation. The clergy of the Abbey continue this tradition today, taking communion out to the ill and the house-bound.

The badly damaged effigies of cross-legged knights in the chancel aisle are thought to represent Thomas of Tyndale and, nearer the east end, Baron GILBERT DE UMFRAVILLE. Tyndale, an early 14th-century knight, has three sheaves on his shield and his legs rest on a lion. Umfraville (1245-1307) was a member of the Anglo-Norman family which built the 12th-century Prudhoe Castle in the Tyne valley not far from Hexham and which played a significant role in the Border skirmishes of the time. Beyond it is the GOOD SAMARITAN WINDOW, installed in 1870. Like some other windows in the Abbey, it had its upper tabernacle-work removed in 1960 and replaced with handmade glass.

BELOW: *The Good Samaritan window is a dramatic combination of 19th century figurework, by the Gothic Revivalist stained glass manufacturer William Wailes, with a rippling, abstract, blue and white background added in the mid-20th century*

OPPOSITE: *Effigy of Gilbert de Umfraville, who was sufficiently devout to found a chantry for two priests to say a daily mass at his family home of Prudhoe Castle*

This Anglo-Saxon chalice, probably used as a portable communion cup, is made of copper-gilt; it is simple in design, with a single fillet of twisted cable decorating the junction of the bowl and the spherical stem

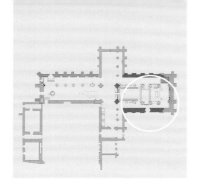

RIGHT: *The Ogle chantry chapel, re-erected between two of the piers of the chancel*

Beyond the Umfraville effigy stands the OGLE CHAPEL, one of two chantry chapels erected inside the Abbey during the 15th century. Set between two of the great piers that frame the chancel and constructed entirely of elaborately carved woodwork, this was founded by a member of the Ogle family, probably Sir Robert Ogle, who died in 1409. The Ogles had been notable in Northumbria since before the Norman Conquest; their main residence was some 15 miles north-east of Hexham, at Ogle Castle. The chapel was dismantled in 1858 and later re-erected, and the woodwork is sadly battered. The triptych, the

BELOW: *The triptych inside the Ogle chantry chapel shows the Resurrection of Christ in the centre; late medieval piety sought redemption through such material expressions of faith*

CHANTRY CHAPELS

These are small chapels built as additions to or inside a church, with an endowment for priests to sing regular masses for the soul of the founder or someone named by him. This practice is based on the medieval belief that the souls of the departed lingered in purgatory, an intermediate state, where they were cleansed of sin and prepared for the kingdom of heaven, and where they could be aided by intercessions from the living. Chantries usually contain the tomb of the founder and are often placed in the chancel. They are a later medieval development, from the fourteenth century onwards, reflecting not only a more personal concern with the welfare of individual souls, but also a sense of the church as representing the whole community of its members, both living and dead.

The effigy of Prior Leschman in his chantry chapel, with his cowl drawn over his eyes

three-part painting at the east end, has the Resurrection at its centre, with the Virgin and St John on either side.

Entering the CHOIR from the south aisle, you enter the liturgical heart of the church, where psalms have been sung and services celebrated down the centuries. Constructed between about 1180 and 1215, its beautiful proportions and architectural detailing make it also the aesthetic heart of the building. One inspiration for the Gothic and related Early English building styles is the sense of God as the source of light, both spiritual and physical. So the outer wall of the church is pierced with tiers of soaring windows, while internal walls are broken up into a series of three superimposed arcades, to let the sunlight, seen as a manifestation of divine grace, stream in.

The aisled choir, with its six bays and three-storey elevation, is characteristically Early English in style. The ground-level arcade is formed of finely moulded pointed arches, while above it the triforium consists of semi-circular arches subdivided by two pointed arches, and above that the clerestory or window arcade has tripartite arcading. The proportions, design and detailing give the choir great dignity and beauty

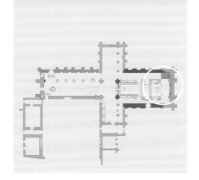

BELOW: *The high altar, with the sanctuary and the great east window behind, part of the restoration work completed in 1908*

The great east window is a 19th-century replacement, built in similar style to the original. The glass, by H.T. Bosdet, dates from 1905 and shows scenes from the life of St Andrew in the upper tier and incidents from the history of the church in Northumbria in the lower. The altar screen, with its great rood or cross above, dates from much the same time, while the painting above the high altar is a copy of one by Andrea del Sarto, c.1505, and shows Mary and the infant Christ meeting Elizabeth and the infant John the Baptist.

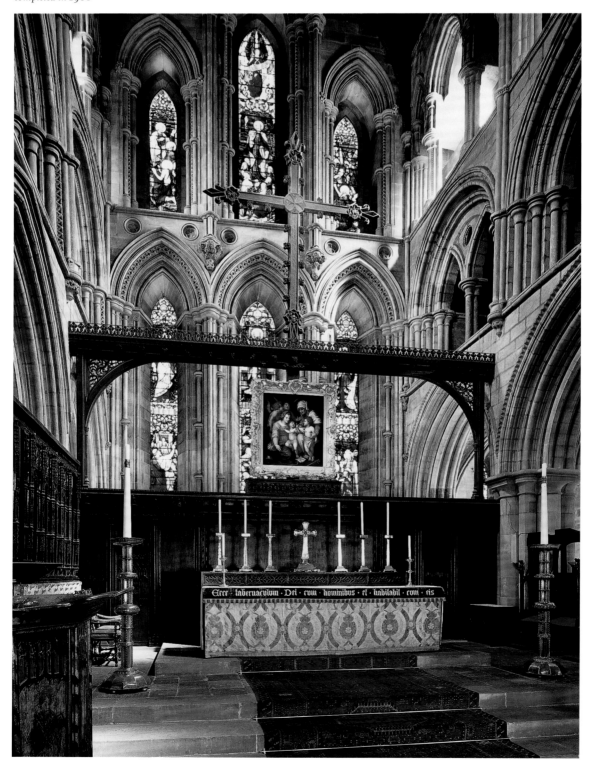

To the right of the high altar is an older survival, the set of five carved oak seats or stalls known as SEDILIA, which were used during services by senior members of the religious community. Sedilia became common in English parish churches from the 13th century; these ones can be dated to the early 15th century by the ornate decoration including a series of small angel figures, one of which carries a shield bearing a hunting horn and three Ws, for William of Woodhorn, who was prior 1409-28.

The LESCHMAN CHANTRY CHAPEL to the left of the high altar is less damaged than the Ogle chapel and contains the tomb of Rowland Leschman, prior 1480-91. The lower part of the chapel walls is stonework, carved with a series of crude, vigorous, almost barbaric, images, some of them surprisingly satirical for the tomb of a prior. This inner wall is decorated with a series of comical or grotesque faces, while the scenes on the outer wall facing on to the aisle include a fox preaching to geese (a common satire on the clergy), a sheep stealer and a jester. Above these on the outer wall are niches containing a series of more traditionally devotional scenes, including St George and the dragon, the Virgin with the crucified Christ, Saints Peter and Paul, and a lily, symbol of purity. The rough stonework contrasts with the particularly fine and delicate tracery of the timberwork above it, but is echoed in the figure that guards the entrance to the tomb, thought to be St Christopher with his staff, patron saint of travellers, whose role is perhaps to guide the prior's soul to paradise. Inside the chapel, the stone altar has five incised consecration crosses, a very rare survival, while above it the reredos, a painted wooden screen, shows Christ's Resurrection (see p.1), with the prior himself kneeling in prayer before it. He appears too in an unusual effigy on his tomb, with his cowl drawn down over his eyes (see p.19).

ABOVE: *These handsome oak sedilia served as seats for the clergy during services*

ABOVE: *The carved stonework of the Leschman chantry chapel's outer wall shows traditional devotional scenes above, with more boisterous and satirical images below*

BELOW: *Details of the Leschman stonework: from left to right, bagpiper, jester, preaching fox and three-headed figure*

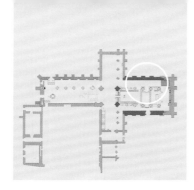

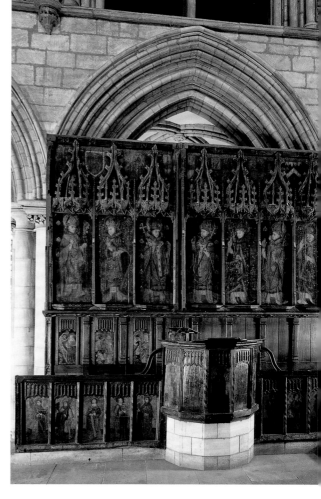

Immediately west of the Leschman chapel, still in the chancel, is a series of 15th-century paintings on wood, relatively rare survivors of the destruction unleashed on church imagery during the Commonwealth period. Although displayed together, these were originally separate items, with different functions. The lowest element is a LECTERN, or reading desk, with a decorated screen, which may have been used for Bible readings during mealtimes in the canons' refectory. Fourteen decorative wood panels show images of Christ, the Virgin and the Twelve Apostles.

Above this is the DANCE OF DEATH, a series of four scenes with a more specifically educational purpose, perhaps a reminder for people of the brevity of life. These show Death, portrayed as a gruesome skeletal figure, dancing before cardinal, king, emperor and pope, a common late medieval allegory

ABOVE: *General view of the series of panel paintings in the chancel, showing the reredos with bishops of Hexham, the Dance of Death, and the lectern and screen. Hexham seems to have been a regional centre for such work, a vigorous and effective form of popular art*

BELOW: *The series of four Dance of Death scenes above the lectern*

emphasizing the irrelevance of rank and power in the face of mortality. Although battered and faded, these still retain an energy and immediacy which testifies to late medieval piety and to the preoccupation with death and the afterworld.

Above this again is a painted screen or REREDOS, which would once have hung above an altar, and which shows seven of the eight canonised Saxon bishops of Hexham, indicating the 15th-century canons' interest in their long Christian heritage. Each bishop is set in a niche with a decorative canopy above, interspersed with shields, one bearing the arms of George Neville, archbishop of York 1464-76, and one the arms of Edward IV (1461-83) in whose reign the reredos was made.

The CHOIR occupies the western end of the chancel. This is where the canons sang the seven daily services, standing throughout as laid down in the monastic rule by which they lived. The CHOIR STALLS you see today are probably 15th century, and include 'misericords' (from the Latin *misericordia*, pity), hinged seats with small ledges on the underside, giving some support to the weary even when the seat is folded up. The carved ends of the stalls and the undersides of the misericords are decorated with biblical and legendary scenes, and charmingly naturalistic flowers and foliage. Today the clergy, together with members of the congregation and visitors, say morning and evening prayer here.

In the centre of the choir stands the FRITH STOOL (see p.5), a Saxon bishop's throne which must date from Wilfrid's church and may indeed have been made for Wilfrid himself. It is carved from a single block of stone, and the incised decoration on the armrests flows from an interlaced pattern symbolizing the Trinity. 'Frith' means peace in Old English; outlaws and fugitives from secular justice could claim sanctuary here. Today, possession of a bishop's throne or *cathedra* is what distinguishes a cathedral from a church. Nearby are the foundations of an apsidal structure, below and therefore pre-dating the chancel floor. At one time this was thought to be the east end of Wilfrid's church (though now believed to be a separate eastern chapel), and so the Frith stool was placed as close as possible to where Wilfrid might once have sat.

BELOW: *Decoratively carved misericords in the choir stalls*

BOTTOM: *This armrest is decorated with the proverbial pelican feeding its young on its own blood, a Christian symbol of the eucharist*

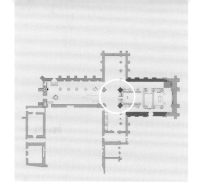

At the west end of the choir, set between the two eastern piers of the crossing and separating the monastic congregation from the lay one in the nave, is a wonderfully crafted wooden ROOD-SCREEN complete with rood-loft or gallery. 'Rood' is the Old English word for a cross or crucifix, and there would once have been a great cross mounted on the rood-loft, marking the ritual threshold between the worldly and the sacred. Today the screen is surmounted by a fine modern organ. On the choir side the screen is decorated with paintings of saints, while the passageway through, under its richly painted ribbed roofwork, bears paintings of the Annunciation and the Visitation. On the nave side, an inscription in the frieze across the main beam asks the viewer to pray for the soul of Prior Thomas Smythson '*qui fecit hoc opus*' – who made this work. Smythson, who was prior between 1491 and 1524, clearly had skilled craftsmen at his command, for the screen is a sophisticated combination of delicate woodwork and painting. On the nave side, 16 richly canopied niches frame painted panels of the bishops of Hexham and Lindisfarne, including Wilfrid and John of Beverley, identifiable by the cross form of the crozier that they carry. Originally this was a closed screen; the four traceried panels were hinged as part of the early 20th-century building work, to integrate the newly-built nave more closely with the rest of the church, reflecting the closer relationship today between congregation and clergy.

ABOVE: *The Annunciation on the north side of the rood-screen's central passage; the red lilies are unusual*

ABOVE: *Detail of the fine rood-screen showing four of the bishops of Hexham. The left-hand panel shows St Cuthbert carrying the head of St Oswald, killed in battle*

OPPOSITE: *Looking west down the choir to the 15th-century rood-screen, with its flaps hinged open to allow a view through to the nave. The modern organ above forms a dramatic and imposing contrast*

THE PHELPS ORGAN

The organ was built in 1974 by Lawrence Phelps and Associates of Pennsylvania, USA. It comprises 34 stops distributed over two manuals and pedals. It is a tracker organ (that is to say, the keys are connected to the pipes by mechanical action). The modern appearance, together with its position on the medieval screen, has not been without some controversy, but it is universally agreed to be a fine musical instrument.

Players are attracted from around the world because of the instrument's particular suitability for the music of Bach, Couperin and their contemporaries. Perhaps surprisingly, however, it has also been well received in works by romantic composers such as Franck, Widor and Reger and by 20th-century masters. During practices, lessons and services, organ music can often be heard in the Abbey, and CDs are available in the Abbey Shop.

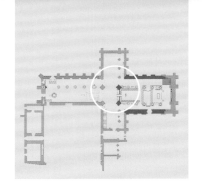

The CROSSING, where the different parts of the church intersect, sets a tone of dignity and monumentality with its tall arches on substantial piers. The short tower above it is decorated on the outside with blind arcades. There is a peal of ten bells; the youngest, hung in 1999, were given the names Millennium and Peace. The pulpit was designed by the architect of the nave, Temple Moore. The crossing is the heart of the liturgical space during Sunday worship; as people come up to take communion and the choir stands behind the round altar, there is a sense of the gathered church coming together.

At the east end of the NORTH AISLE of the chancel, part of the mid-19th century rebuild of the east end, is the CHAPEL OF ST WILFRID, which was dedicated in 1996 and is set aside for private prayer. Also in the aisle is some of the ROMAN AND SAXON CARVED STONEWORK found over the years in and around the church, including a 10th-century coffin lid carved with a long-stemmed cross. Opposite this is a further series of nine 15th-century WOOD-PANEL PAINTINGS, showing scenes from Christ's Passion (see p.11). Like the Dance of Death, these would probably originally have been placed where they could instruct and inspire the congregation. A fine 13th-century ALTAR-TOMB set in the wall between the chancel aisle and the north transept bears a delicately carved image of the Tree of Life. This takes the form of a vine growing from two face-masks, representing Adam and Eve, and ending in a deeply-cut cross formed of vine leaves: both a symbolization of Christ and an affirmation of both the Old and New Testaments as integral parts of the Christian story.

The springing arches and solid piers of the crossing

The NORTH TRANSEPT, like the south, is aisled on the east side only, with elegant rib vaulting forming the roof of the aisle and richly moulded arches separating it from the main body of the transept. The aisle houses the Lady Chapel and a War Memorial Chapel commemorating the dead of World War I. All round the transept at ground level runs a delicate trefoiled arcade, while above on the north and west soar two ranks of slender lancet windows, leading the eye inevitably upwards. The stained glass by William Wailes is a product of the Victorian high church revival. The lower lancets depict the Twelve Apostles bearing their appropriate emblems.

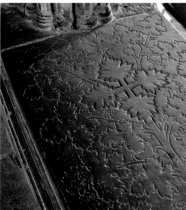

FAR LEFT: *Looking through the curved arch of the altar-tomb in the wall of the chancel aisle to the north transept beyond*

LEFT: *Tree of Life imagery carved on the tomb*

OPPOSITE: *The north transept, with its soaring lancets, complex moulding and trefoil arcading, is Early English building at its best, an impressive and moving expression of faith*

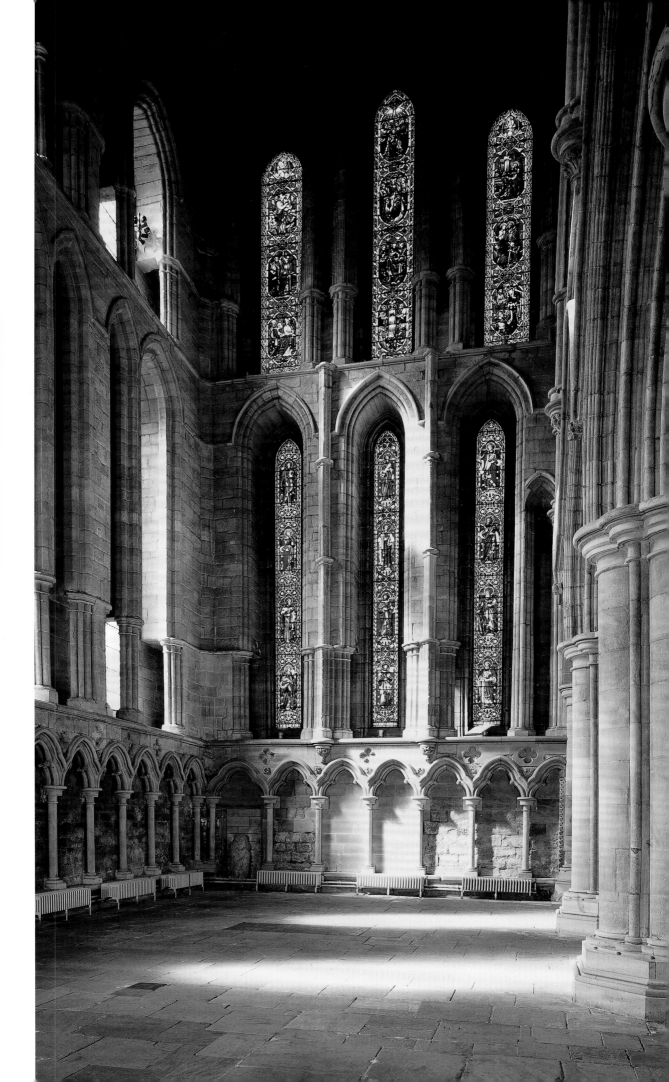

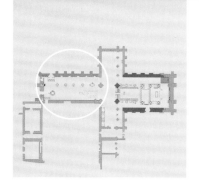

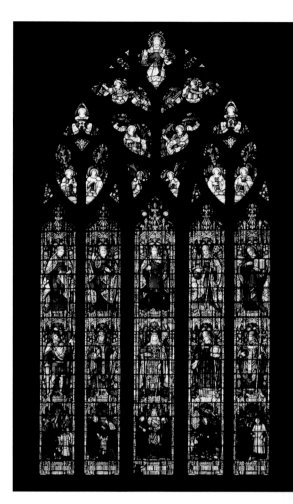

OPPOSITE: *Looking west from the crossing, down the 20th-century nave designed by Temple Moore*

RIGHT: *The great west window, designed by H.T.Bosdet in 1917, shows the Northumbrian saints*

Returning to the crossing, you look west down the pewed NAVE, the newest part of the church. Built in 1907–08 by the architect Temple Moore, an exponent of the popular Victorian Gothic style, it follows the plan of the earlier nave, with a single aisle on the north side. Moore re-used what remained of the 15th-century walls, as you can see on your left, where the older, darker wall rises to a height of several feet. The design of the west end, with its insignificant door where a parish church would normally have a large entrance, emphasizes the primarily monastic function of the church. Rather than copying exactly the architecture of the surviving parts of the church, Moore chose to build the nave in a subdued and tactful version of the 14th-century decorated style, seen most clearly in the stone tracery work in the windows. The great WEST WINDOW, instead of separate lancets as in the transepts, consists of five tall lights branching out into fanciful curvilinear shapes above, all framed by a single arch. The glass, by H.T.Bosdet, has two tiers showing the Northumbrian saints and below them a tier showing episodes from the saints' histories.

The FONT, the place of baptism, or christening, stands on a plinth at the west end of the nave. It is a composite creation which tellingly symbolises the long history of Wilfrid's church. The large circular bowl is believed to be Roman, possibly an inverted pillar-base; it is set on a medieval carved stone base decorated with typically 13th-century dog-tooth decoration; the fine wooden cover is 17th century; while the great canopy above it, more than six metres tall, was made in 1916 by a Belgian refugee, re-using 15th-century woodwork.

Nearby is a glass case containing some of the STONE FRAGMENTS revealed by excavations

for the nave; others are built into the walls or set in purpose-built niches in the aisle. Some of this material is Roman, such as the altar behind the hymnbook stand, but much of it is Saxon architectural work, sections of string-courses, friezes and panels, giving us some idea of the rich relief ornament with which Wilfrid's church was decorated.

The Abbey's education officer with local schoolchildren at the font, learning about the sacrament of baptism. Baptism, the visible and tangible beginning of a Christian life, is powerfully symbolic: the water signifies birth and purification; oil of chrism conveys blessing, joy and empowerment; and a lit candle represents the resurrection of Christ, for whom the baptised are sent out by the congregation to 'shine as a light in the world'

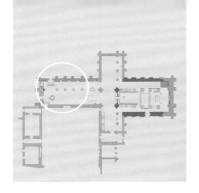

RIGHT: *This rosette carving, unique in England, is a survivor from Wilfrid's church. It is displayed in the sixth niche of the nave aisle*

There is more STONEWORK set into the west and north walls of the NAVE AISLE, including a curved or hogback grave cover, probably late tenth century, with a sharp ridge and a plaited pattern, hinting at Viking influence; a Roman-style rosette pattern; a lively running boar, part of an animal frieze; and sections of a cross-shaft with a richly interlaced pattern in the Lindisfarne style. The BAPTISTRY WINDOW in the west wall shows St Augustine baptizing Ethelbert; Pope Gregory and Anglian slaves; and Queen Bertha praying for Ethelbert's conversion to Christianity. In the middle scene the face of the child in green, facing outwards, is a likeness of the then Rector's daughter Awdrey Savage. Two Armed Services windows in this aisle commemorate the contribution of local people to the achievements of the Royal British Legion and the Royal Air Force, while the last window to the east, commissioned to mark the rebuilding of the nave, celebrates the life of Queen Etheldreda, and incorporates three fragments of Roman glass found at the Corbridge site, the only pre-Reformation glass in the church.

This Roman decorative carving re-used in the walls of the crypt is a reminder of the Abbey's Roman antecedents

In the centre of the nave, you come full circle from 20th-century rebuilding back to Wilfrid's church, with the steep stone stair that descends into the original seventh-century CRYPT. This was discovered only in 1725 when the tower was being reinforced, but would have been the first part of the Saxon church to be built, delved out of the earth before the walls of the main church were erected and bearing out

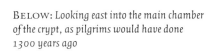

BELOW: *Looking east into the main chamber of the crypt, as pilgrims would have done 1300 years ago*

Wilfrid's biographer Eddius Stephanus' description of 'crypts of beautifully dressed stone'. Like the nave walls, the crypt contains much re-used Roman stone, some with frieze patterns, some with a recurring leaf and berry design, and one slab in the roof (part of which, the 'Geta' stone, is now displayed in the nave) that carries a Latin inscription commemorating the building of a granary by the Emperor Septimius Severus and his two sons in 208 before they marched into Scotland.

The scale and complex plan of the crypt is almost unique in England at this time - only Wilfrid's church at Ripon has something comparable. The closest parallel is

Gregory the Great and the Northumbrian Children in the Slave market at Rome

in Italy, where small tomb chambers similar to the Roman catacombs were constructed to hold the bodies or relics of saints, and churches dedicated to them were built above. At Hexham the stairs lead down into a narrow tunnel-vaulted antechamber which in turn opens through an archway into the main shrine. Two other passages, now blocked, once gave access to the crypt from outside the church, one into the antechamber, one into the shrine itself. We can imagine pilgrims, drawn by tales of relics brought here by Wilfrid, making their way along a dark passage. When they reached the opening of the central chamber, they would see, in the soft radiance from lamp niches set in the walls, a display of the precious relics of the apostle Andrew, a close friend of Jesus himself. Filled with awe and wonder, they would offer a prayer, and then climb the steep steps into the church and the daylight.

Detail from the baptistry window by H.T.Bosdet showing the slave children in the market at Rome, one of them modelled on the then Rector's daughter

TODAY'S CONGREGATIONS AND PILGRIMS join their forebears in being inspired by this place – a place where faith has blossomed, commitments have been made, and where life stories start in hope, are celebrated in joy, and end in grace. As we journey on, the community at Hexham Abbey prays:

Almighty God,
who inspired Saint Wilfrid
to establish a religious community on this site
and to persevere after truth:
help us to know your presence among us now
and guide us as we seek to follow the way of Christ.

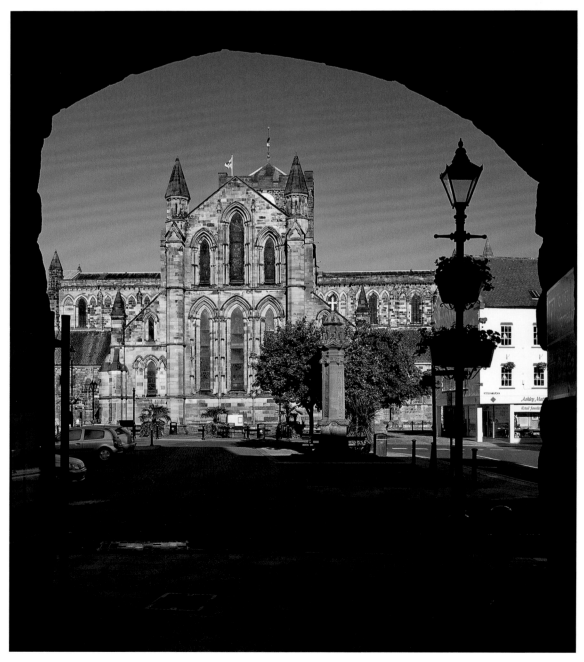

The east end of the Abbey viewed through the arch of the Moot Hall gateway